WALKABOUT

Changing Seasons

© 1993 Watts Books

Watts Books
96 Leonard Street
London EC2A 4RH

Franklin Watts Australia
14 Mars Road
Lane Cove
NSW 2066

UK ISBN: 0 7496 1141 3

10 9 8 7 6 5 4 3 2 1

A CIP catalogue record for this book
is available from the British Library

Dewey Decimal Classification 574.5

Editor: Ambreen Husain
Design: Volume One

Printed in Hong Kong

Photographs: Heather Angel 6, 12, 17
inset, 31; Bruce Coleman Ltd (E Crichton)
18, (P Clement) 21, (H Reinhard) 23; Eye
Ubiquitous (P Prestidge) 4, (Skjold) 30;
Chris Fairclough Colour Library 20, 24;
Robert Harding 7; Frank Lane Picture
Agency (R Wilmshurst) 11, (E & D Hosking)
17, (H Clark) 29; George McCarthy 10;
NHPA (S Dalton) 12 inset, (M Grey) 16,
(G I Bernard) 18 inset; Oxford Scientific
Films (J Hallet) 8, (A Ramage) 9,
(B Milne/Animals Animals) 28 inset; Swift
Picture Library 28, (M King) 5; ZEFA cover,
13, 14, 15, 19, 22, 25, 26, 27.

WALKABOUT
Changing Seasons

Henry Pluckrose

Watts Books

London • New York • Sydney

The cold months of winter
have gone.
It is spring.

What are the signs of spring?
Trees bud and break into leaf.
The sun is higher in the sky.
It does not get dark so early.
The days grow warmer and longer.

Gardens and parks are bright with spring flowers.

Soon, trees are in blossom.

Animals which have rested
through the winter
become active again.
The hedgehog
leaves its winter home
to hunt for food.

Frogs and toads
find water
in which to lay their eggs.

Most birds build nests
to hold their eggs.
The parent birds sit
on the eggs to keep them warm
until they hatch.

When the eggs hatch
the baby birds have to be fed.

Finding food in spring and early summer is much easier than in winter.

Slowly spring becomes summer.
The sun is high in the sky.
The days are longer and
there is more sunshine.
Often the weather is hot
and dry.

Colourful summer flowers
come into bloom.
Trees are full of leaves

and fruit grows fat and juicy
where blossom grew before.

Young animals and birds
leave their nests.
They learn how to find food,
how to climb,
swim
and fly.

Wheat and barley
ripen in the fields.
Summer fruits
are ready to be picked.

As summer ends,
farmers harvest their crops.

Slowly summer becomes autumn.
The days become shorter
and nights are longer.
The sun is lower in the sky.
Cooler weather comes
and many birds fly away
to spend our winter
in warmer countries.

Squirrels, mice and voles
busily gather food
to store away
and use through the winter.

Farmers prepare the fields
for the next crop
in the year which is to come.

Apples and pears are picked and stored…
if they do not get eaten first!

The leaves of many trees
start to turn red, orange,
yellow and brown.

Birds and small animals
feast on autumn berries.
Juicy blackberries grow
on thorny brambles.

Frost sparkles on leaves and branches.
The sun gives little warmth.
Many trees are bare.
It is winter.

Very little grows in winter.
Seeds lie in the cold ground,
waiting for the warmth
of the coming spring.
But the cold does not stop
all flowers from growing…
snowdrops push their way up
even through snow.

It is difficult for animals and birds to find enough food in winter.

Some animals go to sleep. The dormouse finds a warm sheltered place to spend the winter.

A heavy fall of snow
makes everything
look different.
If we wear warm clothes
snow and ice can be fun!

Slowly the seasons change.
Winter is turning into spring.
Plants begin to push up
through the earth.
Animals begin to stir.
Once more it is spring.

About this book

Young children acquire much information in an incidental, almost random fashion. Indeed, they learn much just by being alive! The books in this series complement the way in which young children learn. Through photographs and a simple text the readers are encouraged to comment on the world in which they live.

To the young child, life is new and almost everything in the world is of interest. But interest alone is not enough. If a child is to grow intellectually this interest has to be harnessed and extended. This book adopts a well tried and successful method of achieving this end. By focusing upon a particular topic, it invites the reader firstly to look and then to question. The words and photographs provide a starting point for discussion. Discussion also involves listening. The adult who listens to the young reader's observations will quickly realise that children have a very real concern for the environmental issues that confront us all.

Children enjoy having information books read to them just as much as stories and poetry. The younger child may ignore the written words ... pictures play an important part in learning, particularly if they encourage talk and visual discrimination.

Henry Pluckrose